ROBIN HOOD AND OTHER ITC SWASHBUCKLING COLLECTIBLES

JOHN BUSS

AMBERLEY

First published 2023

Amberley Publishing
The Hill, Stroud
Gloucestershire, GL5 4EP

www.amberley-books.com

Copyright © John Buss, 2023

The right of John Buss to be identified as the
Author of this work has been asserted in accordance
with the Copyrights, Designs and Patents Act 1988.

ISBN 978 1 3981 0870 7 (print)
ISBN 978 1 3981 0871 4 (ebook)

British Library Cataloguing in Publication Data.
A catalogue record for this book is available from
the British Library.

Typeset in 10pt on 13pt Celeste.
Origination by Amberley Publishing.
Printed in Great Britain.

Contents

Introduction

From the mid-1950s to the late 1970s Sir Lew Grade's company ITC (Incorporated Television Company) were quite possibly the most dominant force in British television, but it could be argued that, had it not been for the success of *The Adventures of Robin Hood*, the company would have been little more than a footnote in the pages of history.

Originally formed as the Incorporated Television Programme Company (ITPC) by Grade along with fellow theatre impresarios Prince Littler and Val Parnell, the company soon became dominated by Grade, being renamed as ITC in 1957.

The company had been founded to provide new shows for the fledgling independent television network that was to start broadcasting in 1955. The earliest series from this new company were predominantly swashbucklers or more accurately historical action adventure shows.

Sword of Sherwood Forest, one sheet poster.

The Adventures of Robin Hood was the first of these shows. Proving to be extremely successful both in the UK and USA, it was soon followed by other shows of the same ilk. ITV channels in the UK quickly became dominated by not only Robin Hood, but other ITC programs including *The Adventures of Sir Lancelot, William Tell, The Count of Monte Christo, The Adventures of the Scarlet Pimpernel, The Buccaneers, Sword of Freedom* and the last of ITC's swashbucklers *Sir Francis Drake,* in 1961. All of these shows were turned out almost on a production line, many of the same actors appearing either as regulars or guest stars in several different shows. Some even playing multiple parts on the same show, sometimes even within the same episode.

The biggest problem with a book covering this type of subject is trying to filter which products are actually based upon the television shows concerned; for the most part, these are classic characters of folklore and therefore reside within the public domain. Anybody could then produce or publish a product based upon the said character without paying a licence to the TV company, though if they wished to directly use the actor's likeness from the TV series a licence would need to be taken out. It has been attempted in this book to only include those products that were either licenced or directly relate to the respective television series. In the USA merchandising for many of the shows covered in this book appears to have been handled by Official Films Inc. and USA-produced products for these are normally marked '© Off. F.' or '© Off. Films', while those produced in the UK are marked 'copyright television products limited'.

The Adventures of Robin Hood

This is quite possibly the most fondly remembered of all versions of Robin Hood, starring Richard Greene as the eponymous hero of British folklore. Produced by Sapphire Films for ITC, the series was aimed at the American market and was one of ITC and Lew Grade's first and biggest money spinners. It was also one of the earliest shows to be broadcast on the fledgling ITV network in the UK, first airing only a few days after the service started. Produced on a factory-like production schedule, a 26-minute episode was churned out every four and a half days. In total, over four seasons, 143 episodes were produced. Production was originally based at Nettlefold studios, with very careful angles being used to give the impression of an expansive Sherwood Forest, with the use of one hollow 20-foot tree trunk on wheels, another being built for later series. The shows' theme also became a hit single in the UK charts during 1956, and was as well known as the series itself, still being heard on the radio many years after series had finished.

Once the television series had finished Richard Greene reprised the role of Robin Hood for the big screen in the Hammer Films presentation *Sword of Sherwood*. Strictly speaking, this film has no connection to the series, being made by a different production company and, other than Richard Greene, no other actors from the series reprised their roles.

Books

The Adventures of Robin Hood Number One. The publishers Adprint produced several story books based on the series. While undated, this is from around 1956. The annual has a yellow flash across the top and it contains several text stories and numerous photographs, many being in colour.

The Adventures of Robin Hood Number One.

The following year, 1957, Adprint published *The Adventures of Robin Hood Number Two*. While no writing details are credited in the first book, this second book is credited as being adapted from the series by John Paton. Like the first book, this too is filled with photographs – again, several in colour.

A third book appeared from Adprint in 1958, this time now referred to as being an annual. *The Adventures of Robin Hood Annual No. 3*. Again this had a photo cover, though heavily overdrawn (this time also having a dust jacket of same design), instead of photographs it was instead illustrated throughout by R.S. Embleton, with stories adapted from the series by Arthur Groom.

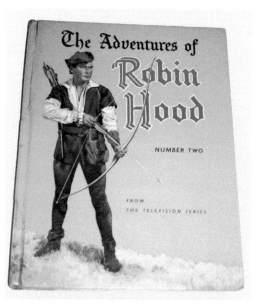

Right: The Adventures of Robin Hood Number Two.

Below left: The Adventures of Robin Hood Annual No. 3.

Below right: The Adventures of Robin Hood Annual No. 4.

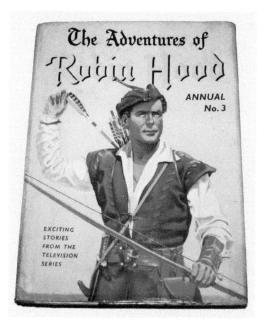

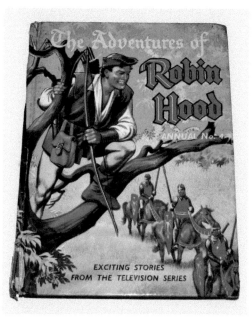

The Adventures of Robin Hood Annual No. 4 appeared in 1959, this time having an illustrated cover, showing Robin waiting in ambush for the Sheriff's men. The stories are by Harold Ramsey, with illustrations by R.S. Embleton.

Another Adprint *The Adventures of Robin Hood* book appeared in 1960. Again R.S. Embleton was the illustrator, with David Leader writing the stories.

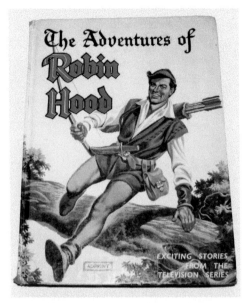

The Adventures of Robin Hood book.

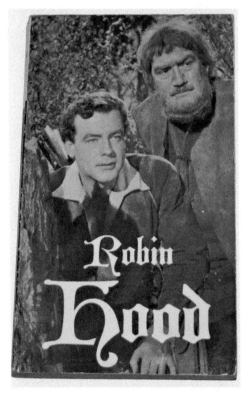

Dutch Robin Hood book.

In the Netherlands the firm of Topaas Reeks published a paperback book of the series in 1964, containing several short stories. There are two editions of this book: one has a photographic cover, the other illustrated, but both contain black and white photographs within the centre.

In the USA as part of their 'Elf' book series the publisher Rand McNally produced *The Adventures of Robin Hood and his Merry Men* in 1955. Published at an original price of 25 cents and intended for junior readers, it was adapted from the series by Bruce Grant with illustrations by William Timmins. This book was also published as a 'giant' book by the same firm.

The *Television Annual for 1956* published by Odhams Press Ltd features a photograph and very small piece on *The Adventures of Robin Hood*. The Amalgamated Press Ltd included a full-page photograph of Richard Greene as Robin Hood in their *TV Mirror Annual 1956*, but no feature.

Undated but believed to be from around 1957 is the *ATV Show Book Number One*, being in the same format as the first Robin Hood book. It is believed that this too was published by Adprint. The book contains a feature, with photographs, on ITC shows entitled 'Cloak and Dagger Heroes', which included Robin Hood.

The comic *Girl,* companion to *Eagle*, published by Hulton Press, included a small feature on Richard Greene and *The Adventures of Robin Hood* in *Girl Film and Television Annual Number 1* was published in 1957. They also included a feature on the new Maid Marion, Pat Driscoll, in the following year's *Girl Film and Television Annual Number 2* in 1958.

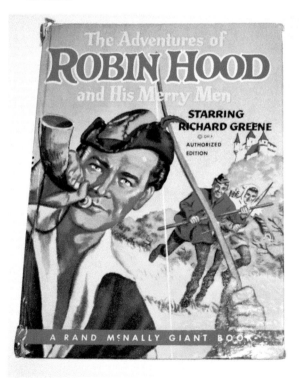

Elf and Giant books' *The Adventures of Robin Hood and his Merry Men.*

In 1959 Adprint did a feature on Robin Hood in their annual *ATV Television Show Book*, while the Purnell *ATV Television Star Book* also included a feature on the series in 1959.

TV Express annual, published by TV Publications Ltd in 1961, had a photographic feature on Robin Hood, while the show is given a passing reference in the *ITV Annual 1964*, also from TV publications Ltd.

Published soon after she had taken over the role of Maid Marion, the book *Making Things with Patricia Driscoll* appeared, published by George G Harrap & Co. Ltd, in 1958. While this book does make a very brief mention of Driscoll's involvement in Robin Hood, it should more correctly be considered to relate to the BBC series *Picture Book*, which she had been best known for up to this point.

Left: Making Things with Patricia Driscoll.

Below: No. 1 Dotto Book and The Robin Hood Painting Book.

Painting books were also produced for the series, which were produced by three firms: Birn Brothers, GFS (Black & Stratton), and Purnell in 1957. *No. 1 Dotto Book* a dot-to-dot book based on the popular quiz/game show of the period, does also feature puzzles related to this series and others.

Toys

Four frame tray jigsaws were produced by Warren Paper Products Co. under their Built-Rite brand in the USA. The set of four 'sta-n-place' puzzles consisted of two portrait images of Richard Greene. A third was an image of Robin in sword combat with an unknown assailant, possibly the actor John Dearth, while the fourth in the set was a group shot of the Merry Men. Issued in 1956, these came packaged in a display box as a set.

Two other frame tray jigsaws were produced by Built-Rite. These are half the size of the other frame tray puzzles. One is a portrait shot of Robin on horseback, while the other shows a green-hooded Robin, again on horseback, with a dismounted Friar Tuck along with another knight. It looks probable that some boxed four puzzle sets contained four large frame puzzles, while later issued sets contained two large puzzles. Two small puzzles as both configurations have been found of these sets. All of these frame puzzles normally had a blue border, but examples of the two smaller puzzles have also been seen with a red border. Built-rite also issued the four large frame puzzle designs as 100-piece Junior Picture Puzzles in a *Famous TV Stars* series of jigsaws, again in 1956.

Built-rite puzzle one.

Above: Built-rite puzzle two.

Left: Built-rite puzzle three.

Built-rite puzzle four.

Box lid for the Built-rite
set of puzzles.

Built-rite puzzle five. (Ralph Cooper)

Built-rite puzzle six. (Ralph Cooper)

Built-rite Junior Picture puzzles.

Two further Built-rite Junior Picture puzzles.
(Ralph Cooper)

15

In the UK it was Tower Press that produced jigsaw puzzles based on the series, all of which featured illustrated scenes. Two 200-piece jigsaws were issued, both approximately 14 x 9 ½ inches in size. The first was 'Robin Sets an Ambush', which shows Robin and his men hiding in the undergrowth while a mounted soldier approaches. The second puzzle in this set is 'Robin Hood Foils the Sheriff of Nottingham', which shows Robin leaping onto a table that the Sheriff is rising from while drawing his sword. As with many Tower Press jigsaws at the time, by sending *6d* to the company you could receive a poster print of the jigsaw's design.

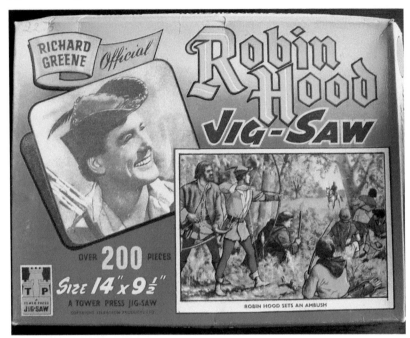

Tower Press jigsaw: 'Robin Hood Sets an Ambush'. (Ralph Cooper)

Tower Press jigsaw: 'Robin Hood Foils the Sheriff of Nottingham'.

Tower Press also issued a set of four 100-piece jigsaws based the series. These were entitled 'The Rescue', 'The Fight in the Forest', 'Robin Tricks the Sheriff' and 'A Feast in the Green Wood'. All six of the Tower Press jigsaws appear to date from around 1957.

Set of four Tower Press 100-piece puzzles. (Ralph Cooper)

Bettye-b Co. in the USA produced a 'Three Dimensional' board game. This featured a colourful vac-formed plastic playing board. It had several so-called magic windows, and switches at the side of the board enabled wheels to be spun underneath, with the spin result being seen through holes.

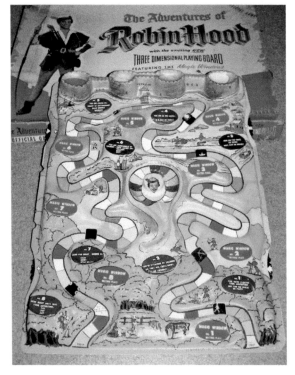

Above and left: 3D board game.
(Bruce Button)

Advert for the 3D board game

In the UK, Bell Toys would produce a board game based on the series. Costing 8/11*d*, theirs was in the form of a race around Sherwood Forest, with every now and then, dependent on the central spinner, a random archery contest. This game was also issued in a box not related to the TV series.

Bell Toys board game.

The playing board for Bell Toys' Robin Hood game.

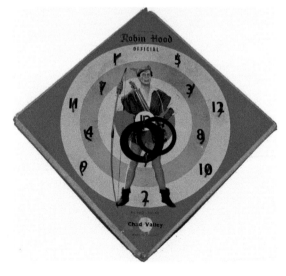

Chad Valley hoopla.

A bit less complicated was Chad Valley's hoopla set, a very simple chipboard target with hooks, for you to throw the five small rubber rings at. The target featured a full-length illustration of Richard Greene as Robin Hood.

Chad Valley were also responsible for producing a shield like badge for Robin Hood, this was sold individually on a backing card and costing 1/6d. The cards featured a small round photograph of Richard Greene with 'Robin Hood copyright television products limited official badge' written above. There appears to be several variations of this item as it can be found in either gold or silver, but also the attached jewel can be either red or blue. To complicate matters further there are also different backing cards. These can be either green or red. These same badges were also issued in the USA, possibly under licence from Chad Valley.

Single shield badge, UK and USA issues.

The USA backing cards do not have a maker's name, just '© Off Films'. Once again there are both green and red backing cards. The US issue also had blue backing cards. The small photograph of Richard Greene is now rectangular, not round like the British issue, and above it is written 'Robin Hood Shield'.

In the USA these were also sold individually from a store display card of twelve. These display cards which feature a full-length photograph of Richard Greene have been seen printed in both red and blue. It is unknown if this second method of sales for the badge was used in the UK.

It must be mentioned that the badges issued in the UK and the USA are actually themselves slightly different in construction. The UK badges have a hinged pin on the rear, while the maker's name, Chad Valley, is also embossed. The USA-issued badges have a solid pin, while '© Off F' is in raised moulding on the badge's reverse.

Store display card for badges as sold in USA. (Vectis)

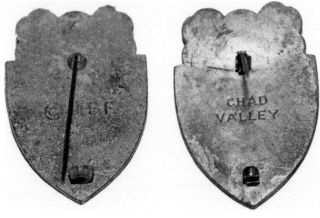

Badge reverse, USA and UK.

22

This badge saw another outlet as part of a set with jail keys. This set consists of the aforementioned badge or shield presented on a backing card with a large metal loop and two die-cast metal keys. These are presented on a shield-shaped backing card with a circular image of Richard Greene being framed by the metal loop for the keys. To the side is written 'Robin Hood Gaol Keys "Jail" & Shield'. The only examples so far seen herald from the USA and while a British issue of this has not been discovered at time of writing, it seems probable that it was issued in this form in the UK as well.

Gaol keys.

Chad Valley shooting game.

Another Chad Valley product was the Robin Hood Shooting Game, a cheaply produced game that had a plastic bow and arrows (produced by DiBro) for firing at card targets representing the Sheriff's men. Robin Hood drawing slates were yet another product to be produced by them.

A masquerade costume was produced in America by Ben Cooper Inc., who were known for producing a vast array of costumes and Halloween accessories/masks. There appear to be two different issues of this costume. The first issue comes in a generic box with no mention of the TV series and the costume is made from a bri-nylon type material, which due to its age is very prone to disintegrate with handling. The second issue box still has a fairly generic lid, showing different characters that the company also made costumes of. The box end now had a drawn image of Richard Greene in the role and copyright details for official films. The first issue of the costume consisted of a one-piece brown top with green sleeves featuring an illustration of Robin Hood on the chest area with attached green trousers. Also included as part of the costume was a brown feathered hat. The second issue of the costume is a two-piece costume and while the green sections of costume are still made from the same nylon-type material as the first issue, the brown sections are made

Chad Valley Drawing Slate. (Ralph Cooper)

Ben Cooper costume, early issue box.

24

from a different material less prone to disintegration. The trousers for this later costume also now had brown boot tops at the bottom.

Much higher quality costumes were also produced for the series by the firm Yanki-boy, who produced two costumes. The first was a Robin Hood one consisting of a hat, jacket, trousers, belt and moneybag. The top had an embroidered Richard Greene badge to the top right. Then a very similar Maid Marion costume, which had a skirt and toy dagger. It is believed that these were sold through catalogue companies.

Right: Ben Cooper one-piece costume. Early issue.

Below left: Ben Cooper costume. Second issue box.

Below right: Ben Cooper two-piece costume, second issue.

Yanki-boy costume advertised in a catalogue. (Ralph Cooper)

Yanki-boy Maid Marion costume. (Ralph Cooper)

Another firm to enter into the costume side of merchandising for Robin Hood was Coleco, who produced a 'ready to wear Archer's Jacket and money pouch'. This came with a leather belt and 'real money'.

A different feathered cap to those offered in the previously mentioned costumes was offered for sale individually by Hugger Caps. This version has a brown rim with an illustration of Richard Greene towards the front on one side, while the central piece is green. What is unknown is whether they were originally sold with a pin badge, as many that are seen on the market now have with them a small round badge. This badge, just over an inch-and-a-half across, has a yellow background and an image of Richard Greene. These badges appear to have been produced by the Green Duck Co., Chicago. Two slight variations of the badge have been noticed: one version has Richard Greene's head and shoulders, while on the other version the image is a little further back, showing him in almost half figure.

To go with their feathered cap, or full Robin Hood masquerade outfit, American children could also purchase the official *Adventures of Robin Hood* archery set, as supplied by the firm Ply-flex. This set consisted of the 'Guaranteed indestructible ply-flex fibre glass bow' with five arrows. This was not a mere toy bow and arrows, but a proper archery set and one can only hope any child lucky enough to own this set was responsible its usage. Toy archery sets were also produced in the UK by the firm Dibro, while in the USA a plastic bow and arrow set was made by Plastics Corp. of West Hempstead.

Coleco Robin Hood jacket.
(Ralph Cooper)

Feathered cap.

27

Green Duck circular badges.
(Ralph Cooper)

Dibro archery set.

Ply-flex archery set. (Vectis)

Marx toys, in the USA, were quick to introduce a Robin Hood set into their range in 1956. They had a castle in their range already, which had been use for an *Ivanhoe* set. This was completely redesigned to become Sherwood Castle, and formed the basis of the new Robin Hood playsets. Marx produced four Robin Hood sets: two generic sets and two based on the television series. The sets for the show contained five character figures based on the likeness of the series' actors: Robin Hood, Maid Marion, Little John, Friar Tuck and the Sheriff of Nottingham. These figures have the character name and '©off. f.' stamped on the base, while the Robin Hood figure also has Richard Greene's name on it as well, but spelt incorrectly as 'Richard Green'. These five Marx figures are incredibly rare compared to the generic figures produced by the company. Aside from the substitution of these figures all of the sets have very similar contents and the two TV show licensed ones only differ from each other in the type of tree included in the set. The playset numbers for these sets are 4721 and 4722 respectively. It is possible that 4721 is the slightly scarcer of the sets as this was a Montgomery Ward catalogue exclusive appearing between June and December of 1956. The boxes for both of these sets are also near identical. The box lid featuring an illustration of Richard Greene only has the code number on box changed.

Right: Marx playset. (Ralph Cooper)

Below: Marx figures. (Ralph Cooper)

Pepys (Castell Brothers Ltd), a firm well known in the UK for producing various playing card games, produced an official Robin Hood card game in 1956, featuring images based on the TV series, while a firm called Ariel also produced a game of Snap cards. This Ariel game is unlicensed, but the box does state 'characters from your favourite TV show'. The cards are all artwork, unlike the Pepys cards, which featured the strange half-drawn half-photographic images which seem to have been very popular at the time.

The Ariel Snap cards open up the debate on products that are related to the series but unlicensed. Up until the 1950s depictions of Robin Hood showed him sporting a beard very similar in style to Errol Flynn, who until this point had been the most commercially successful Robin Hood. Indeed the 1938 Errol Flynn movie was rereleased during the height of the Richard Greene TV series' popularity. So it could be argued that the appearance of many Robin Hood items produced during the 1950s, showing him without a beard, were down to the popularity of Richard Greene in the role. One example of such a product is the range of figures produced by Herald (later taken over by Britain's Ltd). This small range first produced in the late 1950s consisted of Robin Hood, Friar Tuck, Little John and Maid Marion, with a figure of the Sheriff on horseback also being produced. Likewise a similarly sized series of Robin Hood figures also appeared in Kellogg's cereals at around the same period. Pictured here are just two examples of the many generic Robin Hood products to have appeared around this time.

Pepys card game.

Ariel Snap cards. Note that though unlicensed, they mention the TV series on the side of the box.

Trading Cards

A set of sixty cards was issued in the USA by Topps Chewing Gum in 1957. These featured colour photographs of exciting scenes from the series. The cards were sold in two different packs, one costing 1 cent and the other costing 5 cents. It is believed a larger number of cards were included in the more expensive pack.

Topps Gum set.

Topps 1 cent wrapper. (Ralph Cooper)

Topps 5 cent wrapper. (Ralph Cooper)

Also in the USA, Johnson & Johnson issued a set of twenty cards, again in 1957. These also featured colour images from the series and were given away free, one card accompanying a packet of band-aids. These packs had a small promotional splash on the front. You were also able to send off to Johnson & Johnson for a badge that cost 25 cents and needed to be accompanied by a wrapper from any Johnson & Johnson band-aid bandage. As well as the set of picture cards, Johnson & Johnson also produced their own Robin Hood membership cards featuring an image of Richard Greene on the front, with the Sherwood Pledge printed on the rear. These membership cards were the same size as the regular picture cards. It is believed that it was also possible to obtain sets of the cards direct by writing to Johnson & Johnson. Cards that were obtained this way have a perforated edge, rather than a smooth cut edge. In Canada Johnson & Johnson included a set of five iron-on transfers in their band-aids. Once again there was a mail-in offer, this time for a cloth badge.

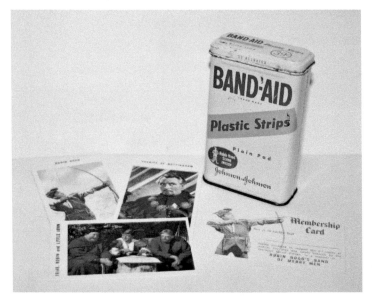

Johnson & Johnson promotional tin with cards.

Johnson & Johnson transfers. (Ralph Cooper)

In the UK, Barratt & Co. Ltd issued packs of sweet cigarettes with cards for *The Adventures of Robin Hood* in 1959. The set of thirty colour photographs features images selected from all four series of the show. The firm also produced an album for you to keep these cards in.

Snap Card Products issued two parallel card sets based on the television game show *Dotto*. One set features a dot-to-dot puzzle, while the other set shows the corresponding actual photograph of the television star or personality that the puzzle is based on. Robin Hood is represented by two cards in both sets, cards 2 show Patricia Driscoll, the second actress to play Maid Marion in the series, while cards 14 are Richard Greene as Robin Hood.

Above: Barratt sweet cigarettes box and cards.

Right: Robin Hood Dotto cards.

ATV Stars card 3.

Colorstars card 3.

Who-z-at Star cards 57 and 15.

Also, from Snap Card, card 3 in the series *ATV Stars series 1* featured Richard Greene and Patricia Driscoll.

The second series of *Colorstars* cards, issued by ABC minors features Richard Greene as card 3 in the set. One of these cards a week was given out to regular ABC Minors cinemagoers in the late 1950s.

Who-z-at Star card 59 and 13.

Mister Softee cards 17 and 23.

The *Who-z-at Star* set of cards from A&BC Gum featured four cards of interest for Robin Hood. This is slightly tricky set to work out. On the front of each card is a different television star, with half of the back being a mini biography of that star. The other half of the cards back is a small photograph of a different star with a clue to who they are, and which card they are on. The cards with a Robin Hood connection are card number 57, which features Richard Greene in the role; he is also referenced on the back of card 15, which featured Dickie Henderson. Then card 59 features Alan Wheatley as the Sheriff of Nottingham, while he is referenced on the back of card 13, Noel Gordon.

TV Personalities, a set of twenty-five cards from the ice-cream firm Mister Softee in 1962, contained two cards for the Robin Hood series. Card 17 featured Patricia Driscoll, while Richard Greene featured on card 23.

Swedish Robin Hood cards.

Tower Press transfers sheet. (Ralph Cooper)

In Sweden a set of *Star Bilder* cards featured Richard Greene as Robin Hood as part of a much larger set of photographs showing various TV and film stars.

Tower Press issued sheets of illustrated transfers in the UK. The sheet features thirty-two square transfers based on scenes in the series.

In Argentina a circular card, possibly a milk bottle cap, appeared featuring Richard Greene as Robin Hood. This was part of a much larger series, which seems to have included images from almost every TV series of the 1950s and 1960s. Japanese-issued photographs have also been seen but the origin of these is unknown.

Magazines/Comics

In the UK, the publishing firm Pearson, as part of their *TV Picture Stories* series of digest comics, published three titles based on episodes of the series. These comics had the same title as the episode they were based upon. The first in the series was *The Moneylender*, which appeared in March of 1959, as did *Friar Tuck*. The final title from Pearson was, *A Husband for Marian*, which appeared in August of 1959.

Friar Tuck and *The Moneylender* comics.

A Husband for Marian comic. (Steven Taylor)

In the USA, several different comic book publishers produced their own versions of Robin Hood comics, but only one was actually licenced for the series. A firm called Magazine Enterprises, who were already producing a quarterly Robin Hood title, introduced photographic covers of Richard Greene in issue six, with the characters being altered to resemble the actors on the show. Only three issues of this now 'official' Robin Hood comic appeared before the series ended. The artwork in these issues was by Frank Bolle and Bob Powell.

At least one issue of the *TV Times* magazine – the featured Robin Hood on its cover. The issue dated 7 October 1955. This was only the third ever issue of the magazine, ITV having started broadcasting on 22 September, and as well as featuring the series on its cover, it also included a feature on the making of the show. The 1957 Christmas special from *TV Times* featured the new Maid Marion, Patricia Driscoll, on its cover.

Richard Greene, in his guise as Robin Hood, along with Bernadette O'Farrell as Maid Marion, would also make it onto the cover of the American *TV Guide* dated 12–18 May 1956. Two previous issues had features on the series; the first, in the 24 September 1955 issue, included it as part of its Fall Preview of new shows. While the other from 12 November 1955 had a very small feature.

Above: ME Comic 6, 7 and 8.

Left: TV Times cover.

TV Times Christmas special 1957.

TV Guide cover.

Seattle TV Prevues cover and
French *Télé 7 Jours* cover.

The TV supplement 'Seattle TV Prevues' of the *Seattle Post Intelligencer*, featured the first Maid Marian (Beradette O'Farrel) on the cover of its issue dated 25 March 1956. Then, with French broadcasts of the series underway, *Télé 7 Jours* featured the series on its cover in 1965.

Records

Several versions of the theme tune appeared as singles around the world. In the USA a version of the theme was released on the Coral label (Coral 9-61526) recorded by Alan Dale with the Dick Jacobs Orchestra in 1955. Coral also released this single in Australia the same year as Coral CS-866.

In the UK the theme was released as a single by both Dick James, with the Ron Goodwin Orchestra, and Gary Millar. Both versions of the theme entered the UK charts in January 1956. Dick James' version, released on a 10 inch 78 rpm shellac single by Parlophone (R4117), reached a peak position of 14. This did also see issue on the new 7 inch 45 rpm format as well (Parlophone MSP 6199), which is much scarcer. The Gary Miller version also released as a 10 inch 78 rpm single, and fared slightly better in the charts, reaching a high position of 10 on 9 February 1956. Gary Miller's version was recorded with Tony Osborne and his orchestra, and was released by Pye Nixa (N15020).

Dick James theme 78. (Robert Girling)

Gary Miller theme 78. (Robert Girling)

Nelson Riddle theme 78.

Capitol records in the USA released a version of the theme recorded by the Nelson Riddle Orchestra. This recording saw several different releases around the world both as a 45 rpm single and as a 78 rpm single in 1955. The initial USA release appears to have been on a 45 rpm Capitol F3287, with a 78 rpm release as 3287, while in the UK it was a 78 rpm CL14510. The 45 rpm version was also released in Japan (CEC-13) and Germany (CF 3287), while it was released as a 78 rpm single in both New Zealand and the Netherlands, both Capitol 3287.

Frankie Laine recorded a rendition of the theme on Columbia J4-275. His version was released in a picture sleeve in 1959, with the reverse being his rendition of 'Champion the Wonder Horse'. This was issued both on a 78 and a 45. Yet another American issue of the theme came on RCA Victor (47-6308) in 1955, this time recorded by Joe Reisman's Orchestra and chorus.

In New Zealand a group called, The Three Lads released their version of the theme on the label Tanza (Z282). In Denmark, on Decca 45-F-10682, in 1956, a version recorded by Billy Cotton and his Orchestra saw release with a picture sleeve as a 45 rpm single. Canada also saw its own version of the theme released; this issue was by Sparton of Canada Ltd (4-224R) in 1956, being recorded by Bob Dale.

Another cover version of the theme was by Ronnie Ronalde with the Norrie Paramor Orchestra and chorus, which was released as a 78 rpm single in the UK on the Columbia label (DB3734) in 1955.

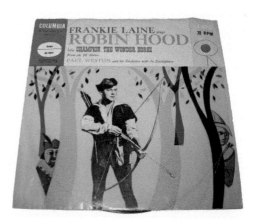

Frankie Laine picture sleeve.

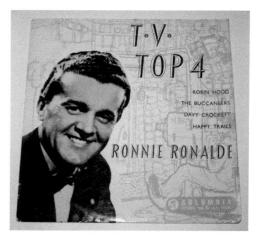

Ronnie Ronalde *TV Top 4* EP.

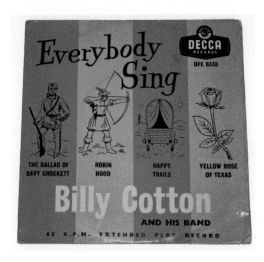

Billy Cotton *Everybody Sing* EP.

Several of these different recordings of the Robin Hood theme also appeared on extended playing records. Gary Miller's version appearing on his EP *Four Big Hits* in 1956, which was released as Pye Nixa NEP 24013.

An EP of four TV themes, *T.V. Top 4* was released on Columbia records (SEG 7784) by recording artist Ronnie Ronalde. He was accompanied by orchestra and chorus conducted by Norrie Paramour for his rendition of Robin Hood. No year of release is given on the record, but it would date from around 1958.

Everybody Sing, an EP from Billy Cotton and his Band released on the Decca label (DFE 6338), featured a rendition of the Robin Hood theme along with 'Ballad of Davy Crocket'.

The Nelson Riddle EP *Lisbon Antigua* featured Riddles' recording in 1956. This was released on the Capitol label (EAP1-710).

Only Gary Miller's recording of the theme appears to have been included on an LP, which was the *Hit Parade of 1956* released by Pye Nixa (NPT 19015). Strangely this LP is a 10 inch record rather than the usual 12 inch.

Miscellaneous

A slightly strange item to be marketed for a medieval folk hero was a children's wristwatch as produced by Bradley in 1956. This originally sold originally for $4.95, though the price later rose to $6.45. The watch had a lozenge-shaped dial and featured a full-length illustration of Robin Hood drawing his bow. A slightly later issue of the watch was sold with Cufflinks and Tie-clip for $7.95. This same watch had previously been sold as related to the 1952 Walt Disney film version of *Robin Hood*.

Another slightly strange product was the Robin Hood guitar, produced by Range Rhythm toys and available in two different colours. A more understandable product came from the J. W. Johnson Company of Bellwood Illinois, who produced an umbrella tent in 1955. This came complete with Robin Hood graphics printed upon its side.

Sheet music of the series theme by Carl Sigman was released in the USA, UK and Australia. In the USA it was published by the Official Music Co., Inc., while in the UK the release was by New World Publishers Ltd and the Australian issue was Southern Music

Tent. (Ralph Cooper)

Wristwatch.

UK, Australian, USA and seventies re-issue sheet music.

Publishing Co. All three issues had very similar green-coloured covers showing Richard Greene in the role. There appear to have been two issues of the Australian release, the second issue having an increased price and different back cover, while a latter UK issue of the music features an abstract cover rather than an image from the series.

A rarely seen item of merchandise for the series are the disposable paper cups that were produced for the series by the firm Lily in the USA. Two versions were marketed 'Hot cups', which came with fold-out handles and were sold boxed in packs of fifteen cups with stylised illustrations around the cup sides, and 'Cold cups', which featured the same stylised illustrations but lacked the fold-out handles and came in packs of twenty-five. It is quite possible that other paper party wear like this was also produced by the firm.

Hot cups. (Vectis)

Lily cups box reverse.

A range of premiums were available from Lily by sending off tokens from the box tops. These included what they called their '3 piece set', which featured a rubber dagger, silver Robin Hood badge and a real feather along with instructions for making your own Robin Hood hat. If you didn't want to make your own hat, you could send for a ready-made one for the cost of one box token and 60 cents. If you didn't fancy a hat, it was possible to get a wallet with a full-colour picture of Robin Hood printed upon it, for only 50 cents and the obligatory box token.

Knife, feather and shield set. (Ralph Cooper)

Money pouch. (Ralph Cooper)

The premiums didn't stop there. Also available from Lily were plastic bow and arrow sets, a green 'suedette jerkin', a bolo tie with metal Robin Hood slide, and a printed Robin Hood pouch with '6 genuine foreign coins'. All of these for box tokens and just a few cents. It is probable that most, if not all, of these premiums were pre-existing products from other firms. Certainly the money pouch with coins was marketed by a company called Royal.

In Canada, a series of eight glasses, sized approximately 4.5 inches tall and 2.5 inches in diameter, were produced by Federal glass, each featuring the likeness of a different character from the series. These glasses were apparently a premium available with peanut butter. It seems that the peanut butter would be sold within the glass, which when empty could then be used to drink from. The eight glasses in the set were: Robin Hood, Sheriff of Nottingham, Friar Tuck, Little John, Maid Marion, Will Scarlet, Prince John and King Richard. Each glass also bore the name of the character below the image, and the rear of the glass featured the image of a feathered hat with the number the glass was in the set. The printed likenesses were for the most part very good representations of the actors in the series.

Peanut butter glasses, Robin Hood and Maid Marion.

Peanut butter glass, Little John.

Johnson & Johnson were one of the sponsors of Robin Hood on American television, and as well as the promotional set of cards mentioned earlier they also produced a small ceramic figurine of Friar Tuck carrying Robin on his back as a promotional gift. Another of Robin Hood's sponsors on American television was Wildroot hair tonic. Wildroot produced a Pewter goblet with 'Robin Hood' engraved on its side; there is however no mention of the series or copyright on this item. The company also produced Robin Hood hair tonic, the bottles of which likewise do not acknowledge the TV series. The series was however used in the firm's advertising and their Wildroot Cream-oil Hair Tonic bottles did come in a photographic box showing both Richard Greene and Bernadette O'Farrell in the series. The firm also issued promotional postcards and a double set of playing cards featuring the actors to commemorate them visiting the USA on a promotional tour.

Huntley & Palmers, the biscuit company, produced a small round biscuit tin with a photograph on its lid showing Richard Greene in his role as Robin Hood. The offset litho-printed tin was manufactured by Huntley Boorne & Stevens, with the tins base being embossed 'Huntley and Palmers Biscuits'.

Right: Wildroot Cream-oil box.

Below: Wildroot playing cards. (Ralph Cooper)

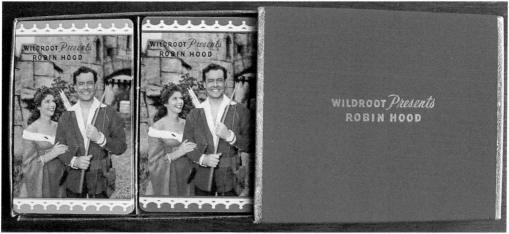

Wildroot display stand. (Ralph Cooper)

Huntley & Palmers biscuit tin.
(Stephen Brown)

Cottage cheese tops. (Ralph Cooper)

Kydd's Dairy, of Lowell Massachusetts, on its packets of 'Creamed Cottage Cheese', featured several different mail-in offers upon the lids. Interestingly, the same offers appeared on the Lily paper cups.

Two sets of film strips were issued by Film Stips. These featured photographic images from the series (effectively a strip of 35 mm slides), one of which was entitled *The Coming of Robin Hood* and the other *Robin Hood and Sudden Death*.

The Bondex company issued an iron-on patch for the sum of 10 cents. This was around 3 x 4 inches in size, featuring a drawn image of Richard Greene. Croydon Inc. produced a plastic Robin Hood wallet in 1956.

In France, key rings with a plastic fob encasing a photograph of Richard Greene were produced in the early 1960s. These appear with at least three different coloured backgrounds – yellow, blue or red. Also appearing in France around this time were several postcards showing photographs from the series.

Robin Hood and Sudden Death film strip.

Iron-on badge.

French key ring, front and reverse.

49

The Adventures of Sir Lancelot

This thirty-episode series produced between 1956 and 1957 follows in the style of many other of the ITC shows from the period. Sir Lancelot, played by William Russell (later one of *Doctor Who*'s first companions), is the famed knight of the Round Table having to stave off threats to the throne by marauding invaders. This is one of the earliest British television series made, at least partially in colour, with the final fourteen episodes being filmed entirely in colour. The show was, again, made by Sapphire Films for ITC, and likewise made use of many US writers blacklisted in their home country. Ronald Leigh-Hunt played King Arthur for the majority of the series, Bruce Seton having occupied the role for the first three episodes. Queen Guinevere was played by Jane Hylton, while Cyril Smith appeared as Merlin the Magician, with whom Sir Lancelot would often conspire in ways to thwart whatever threat was endangering Camelot.

Books

Adprint produced a hardback storybook, *The Adventures of Sir Lancelot,* adapted from the series by John Paton. Photographs, some colour, appear throughout. This undated publication is believed to be from 1957.

The Adventures of Sir Lancelot.

The Adventures of Sir Lancelot No. 2.

50

Another hardback storybook, *The Adventures of Sir Lancelot No. 2*, appeared in 1958. Again published by Adprint, this book had a photo cover with a dust jacket of the same design and stories adapted from the series by Arthur Groom, and illustrated throughout by R.S. Embleton.

In the Netherlands, Topaas Reeks published a paperback book based on the series in 1964 containing six short stories and black and white photographs from the series. There are two editions, one with photographic cover and the other with an illustrated one.

Whitman Publishing USA, as part of their 'Big Little Book' series, published *Sir Lancelot* by Dorothy Haas and illustrated by Helmuth Wegner in 1958. In 1963 a soft-covered story book for the series, *Lancelot*, was published in France.

Dutch Sir Lancelot book.

Whitman Big Little Book.

French Sir Lancelot storybook.

The feature entitled 'Cloak and Dagger Heroes', in the undated *ATV Show Book Number One*, believed to have been published by Adprint, includes *The Adventures of Sir Lancelot* with photographs. Hulton Press included a photograph of William Russell, as Sir Lancelot, in a feature on fan mail in their 1959 *Girl Film and Television Annual Number 3*.

Birn Brothers Ltd produced two different painting books for the series in 1957, while the show was also represented in the *RCA Coloring Book*.

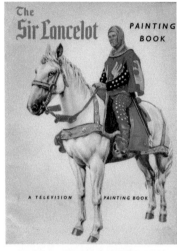

Painting book. (Steven Taylor)

Painting book. (Ralph Cooper)

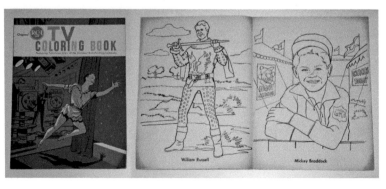

RCA colouring book and contents.

Toys

A 500-piece jigsaw puzzle by Tower Press, approximately 20 ½ x 15 inches in size, shows a photograph from a high angle of the knights seated around the Round Table.

An illustration of this scene was used as the box design for a board game produced in the USA by Lisbeth Whiting Co. in 1957. The box lid also featured a 'film strip' of photographs from the series down the lid's right-hand side. This incredibly rare game was issued in the UK by Bell Games in 1959, appearing to have had all references to the TV series removed. It is instead just produced as a generic Sir Lancelot game. The box lid for the UK version carries the same artwork, as does the playing board, but the strip of photographs has now been removed, replaced by an illustration of Camelot and Sir Lancelot's shield.

Masquerade costumes by Ben Cooper have been seen, but they don't appear to have been licenced for the series.

Sir Lancelot jigsaw.

Sir Lancelot board game, British issue.

Trading Cards

While *The Adventures of Sir Lancelot* does not appear to have had its own dedicated trade card set, at least the following card sets contained cards relating to the series. As part of a larger set of cards relating to various different series, Snap Card Products issued two cards relating to the show in its first *ATV Stars* set: one card of William Russell, card 34, then card 42 showing Jane Hylton as Queen Guinevere. Card 62 in the *Who-z-at Star* set, also from Snap Card Products, featured William Russell, who also featured on the reverse of card 10, Tommy Cooper. The ice-cream company Mister Softee produced a set of *TV Personalities* cards in 1962, which also contained William Russell as Sir Lancelot on card 21.

Sir Lancelot snap cards.

Who-z-at Star card 62 and 10

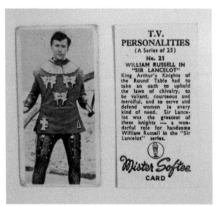

Mister Softee card 21.

In the USA, the Dell publishing group, as part of their 'Dell Four Color Comic' series, published *Sir Lancelot and Brian* in 1957. The cover featured images from the series and two stories, 'The Knight of the Red Plume' and 'The Ferocious Fathers'. The original cover price was 10 cents, but it can also be found with the Canadian price of 15 cents. This title was republished in the UK by World Distributors Ltd as No. 27 in their 'A Movie Classic' series of comics priced at 1/-.

The Adventures of Sir Lancelot featured on the cover of the *St Louis Post – Dispatch TV Magazine* for 11 November 1956. A short feature on both the actor and new series appeared within.

The *Sunday Star TeleVue* TV listings magazine in the Washington DC region of the USA dated 9–15 December 1956 featured William Russell on the front cover and in a small feature within. Another cover appeared on the 6 January 1957 edition of the *Chicago Sunday Times TV Prevue* magazine, and *Tele Magazine* in France also featured the series on its cover in 1962.

USA and British comics.

St Louis Post TV Magazine and *The Sunday Star TeleVue* covers.

A series of Dutch comics were produced that featured an illustrated version of one of the series publicity photographs on each cover. Several of the issues feature adaptations of episodes. Running from 1961 until 1987, a series of French *Lancelot* comics appeared, and the first eighteen issues feature photographic covers from the TV series.

Records

A 7 inch 45 rpm single of the series theme 'The Ballad of Sir Lancelot' was released in the USA (MGM K12358) with the theme from another ITC series, *The Buccaneers,* on the reverse. Recorded by the group The Naturals it was released in a picture sleeve depicting both series. These recordings saw issue in the UK as a 10 inch 78 rpm demo record (MGM 939).

Early issues of the French Sir Lancelot comic.

Sir Lancelot theme single.

Miscellaneous

In the Netherlands various items were produced. Postcards of photographic scenes from the series were produced in both colour and black and white. The colour cards have the appearance of being black and white images that have been over-coloured. Some, though not all, bear the name Gebr. Spanjersberg N.V., Rotterdam, while the black and white postcards are marked Filmpers P.O.B.521, Amsterdam. It is possible that cards were also produced by Hercules, Haarlem (b/w postcards), Uitgeverij Spanjersberg Rotterdam and Uitgeverij Takken from Utrecht.

A popular giveaway with groceries were small metal pins, almost like a tiepin, which featured various different images. Three different coloured metal pins were produced featuring an image of William Russell as Sir Lancelot. A white plastic pin also appeared bearing an image of Sir Lancelot. Matchbox labels also seem to have been popular in the Netherlands, with a vast array of different actors' images appearing on labels, including William Russell.

A 35 mm film strip entitled *Sir Lancelot "the Challenge"* was also produced.

Above left: Dutch postcards.

Above right: Dutch pins.

Right: Dutch matchbox label.

The Adventures of the Scarlet Pimpernel

Produced by Towers of London for ITC in 1955 and broadcast in 1956, this is one of the earliest of ITC's shows in this book. Created by Michael Hogan it ran for eighteen episodes. Marius Goring, also having a producing credit, reprises his dual role of Sir Percy Blakeney aka the Scarlet Pimpernel, previously played on radio in 1952.

A 1903 stage play by Baroness Emmuska Orczy before being turned into a novel in 1905, the Scarlet Pimpernel went on to appear in a series of further novels. Set in revolutionary France, he is a forerunner to many a superhero with a secret identity enabling him to carry out his heroic deeds. Often at odds with Citizen Chauvelin, portrayed by Stanley Van Beers, he sets about rescuing French aristocrats from the infamous guillotine aided by Sir Andrew Ffoulks, played by Patrick Troughton (the future Second Doctor in *Doctor Who*), who appears as a guest star in many ITC shows of this period.

Related Products

Thus far, only four commercially released products containing any reference to the series have been discovered. *The Television Annual for 1956* published by Odhams Press Ltd and the *TV Mirror Annual 1956* from the Amalgamated Press Ltd both feature a photograph and small piece on the TV series. A small piece and two photographs are in the undated *ATV Show Book Number One* as part of the 'Cloak and Dagger Heroes' feature.

The Snap Card Products set of *ATV Stars series 1* includes Marius Goring as Sir Percy Blakeney on card 39.

Above Left: Contents of *The Television Annual for 1956* showing both Robin Hood and the Scarlet Pimpernel.

Above Right: ATV Stars card 39.

The Buccaneers

Action and adventure on the high seas came in this ITC series featuring Robert Shaw as Dan Tempest. Another series produced for ITC by Sapphire Films, between 1956 and 1957, this is slightly unusual in that the main star, Captain Tempest, doesn't appear in the first two episodes. These instead tell the story of how Governor Woodes Rogers, played by Alec Clunes, purged the pirates from their Caribbean stronghold, which Tempest had virtually ruled. His pirating now pardoned, Tempest is a king's man, standing with the new governor against a common enemy – the Spaniards.

Books

An annual-sized storybook by Adprint, while undated it is believed to have been published in 1958. This, as with others by Adprint, contains a large selection of photographs from the series; several in colour together with stories adapted from the series by John Paton.

The 'Big Little Book' series of books from Whitman Publishing in the USA includes a 1958 book, *The Buccaneers*, written by Alice Sankey and illustrated by Russ Manning.

The undated *ATV Show Book Number One*, believed to have been published by Adprint, contains a feature with photographs on ITC shows including *The Buccaneers,* entitled 'Cloak and Dagger Heroes'. This makes interesting reading, as it states that the show's star Robert Shaw was 'now under a seven-year contract' despite the series only being produced for two years.

Purnell & Sons published a painting book based upon it in 1957, featuring drawings by Shelia Findlay.

No. 1 Dotto Book contained dot-to-dot puzzles for the series.

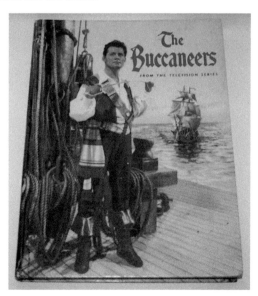

Buccaneers annual.

Big Little Book.

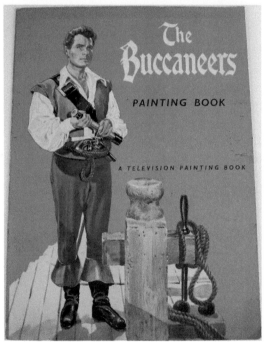

Painting book. (Steven Taylor)

Toys

American toy company Transogram produced several products based on the *The Buccaneers*. A board game for up to six players in 1957, it features a colourful board depicting the high seas with several islands and promotes itself as 'a sea-faring game of adventure'.

A Sling Dart Game consisting of a target depicting four ships around a treasure chest that could either be hung up or positioned with a stand, a catapult or slingshot, and three suction-tipped darts was sold in a bag with header card. The target was produced from a printed piece of hardboard and given the fancy name 'Masonite'.

Effectively the same toy was also sold as Sling Darts. The primary difference being that the target, depicting a single ship, was now formed from the cardboard backing board that the darts were sold on.

Tower Press are believed to have produced two 200-piece jigsaws approximately 14 x 9½ inches in size based upon the series, one being entitled 'To the Rescue'. These came in the one-piece end-opening style of box.

Newark Felt Novelty USA produced several items including an official *Buccaneers* black felt hat, with an image of Dan Tempest printed on the front, 'made of 100% new wool-blend felt'. These were sold loose with a variety of colourful plumes.

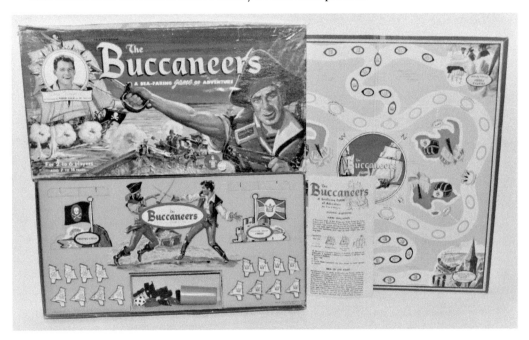

Above: Transogram board game based on the series.

Right: Toy trade publication from 1957 showing Robert Shaw with a copy of the game.

BUCCANEER Robert Shaw (left), who stars as Dan Tempest on the CBS-TV adventure series, gathers some prize booty from Charles S. Raizen, president of Transogram, in the form of the new Buccaneers game. The 4-color boxed $1.98 retailer is a sea-action board game of strategy and skill. The television series is scheduled for a full year's run.

TOYS *and* NOVELTIES—*March*, 1957

Left: Sling dart game.

Below: Sling dart 'Masonite' board.

Trade advert for a felt hat.

Trade advert for *Buccaneers* set.

Buccaneers shooting game. (Steven Taylor)

The hat was also part of the 'Official Dan Tempest "*The Buccaneers*" Kit', which included a toy flintlock pistol, 19-inch-long plastic cutlass, a pull-out telescope with compass, and a black eye patch. A fine selection for any budding young swashbuckler, it is unknown if any of these products other than the hat were available to purchase separately.

Chad Valley produced a rather crude shooting game containing a pair of wire-sprung-loaded pistols, which could fire small wooden beads at card targets. Four cartoon-like targets featuring images of pirates were included, and the box features a colourful if somewhat naïve painting of Robert Shaw as Dan Tempest. Compared to the American products for the series, this has a cheap hastily put together feel about it.

Trading Cards & Miscellaneous

Snap Card Products featured at least two relevant cards in a larger set of cards relating to various different series. In the set *ATV Stars series 1*, card 29 shows Robert Shaw in the series while card 30 out of the set of fifty cards depicts George Margo. The set of twenty-five *TV Personalities* cards from Mister Softee featured Robert Shaw in *The Buccaneers* on card 22.

A 35 mm Film Stips set was issued featuring photographic images from the series entitled *The Ghost Ship*. Sheet music of the theme appeared, being published by Chappell & Co. Ltd in 1956.

ATV stars cards 29 and 30.

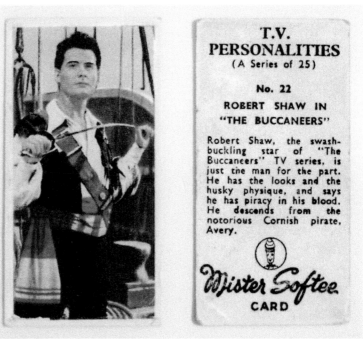

Mister Softee card 22.

Above: *The Buccaneers* film strip.
(Ralph Cooper)

Left: *The Buccaneers* sheet music.

Magazines/Comics

In 1957 publishers Dell produced a comic based on the series, No. 800 in their 'four color comic' series it featured a full-length story, 'Captain Dan Tempest'. World Distributors Ltd republished this under licence in the UK as No. 33 in their 'Movie Classic' line in the same year. This one shot comic adapts the first three episodes, altering the order slightly by starting with the show's third episode, then recounting earlier events as a flashback.

Pearson once again published several digest-sized comics in its *TV Picture Stories* series. The first based on *The Buccaneers* was *The Wasp,* which appeared in February of 1959. The second, *The Gunpowder Plot,* appeared in March. One more comic based on the series, *Dead Man's Rock,* was published in Pearson's larger American comic book sized title *TV Photo Stories* in 1960. As with all the others, these stories were based upon episodes of the same name within the television series. One issue of a *Dan Tempest* comic, possibly a reprint of a Pearson comic, appeared in Spain.

USA and UK version of Dell's comic.

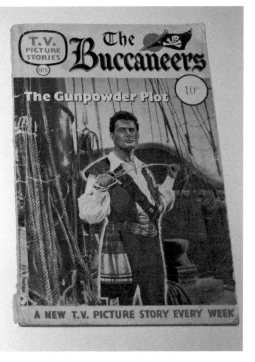

TV Picture Stories *The Wasp* and *The Gunpowder Plot*.

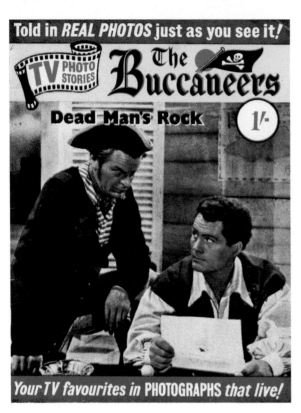

Dead Man's Rock. (Steven Taylor)

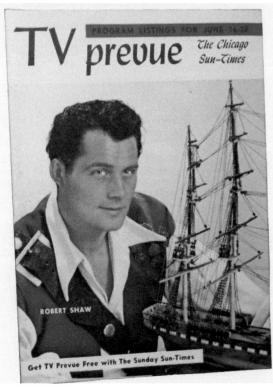

Buccaneers *TV Prevue* cover.

While a feature about the series was included in an issue of the USA *TV Guide* dated 19 January 1957, it was not on the cover. *The Buccaneers* did however feature on the cover of the *Chicago Sunday Times TV Prevue* magazine for 16 June 1957.

Records
A single of the series theme was released by The Naturals along with the 'Ballad of Sir Lancelot'. For full details, see page 56.

A cover version by Ronnie Ronalde with the Bill Shepard Chorus and Orchestra was released as a 78 rpm single in the UK on Columbia DB 3892, also appearing on the EP *T.V. Top 4* released on Columbia Records (SEG 7784). Tracks on the record included 'Robin Hood', 'Ballad of Davy Crocket' and 'Happy Trails' from the *The Roy Rogers Show*.

Buccaneers theme single.

Buccaneers Ronnie Ronalde
78 rpm single.

The Count of Monte Cristo

Based on the characters of the Alexander Dumas novel, this ITC series, a co-production with Television Programs of America, Inc., ran from 1956 to 1957. American actor George Dolenz (future Monkee Mickey Dolenz's father) stars as Edmond Dantès, the self-styled Count of Monte Cristo. Set during the 1830s restoration period of the French monarchy, it follows his continuing adventures after the events of the novel. Running for thirty-nine episodes, early episodes of the series were filmed in the USA at the Hal Roach studios before moving to the UK. Also in the series were Nick Cravat as his mute sidekick Jacopo, and Robert Cawdron as Rico.

Books

Only three items referencing *The Count of Monte Cristo* have thus far been found. The undated *ATV Show Book Number One* sees the show represented as part of the 'Cloak and Dagger Heroes' feature, a full-page photograph of George Dolenz in the lead role, and a small photograph on the cover. A book released for the TV quiz/gameshow *Dotto* contains a reference in the form of a dot-to-dot puzzle.

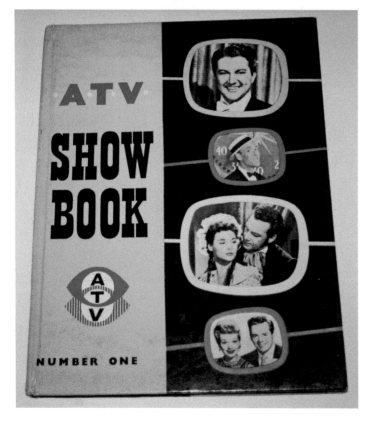

Count of Monte Cristo on the cover of *ATV Show Book Number One* (third image down).

In the second series of *ATV Stars* from Snap Card Products, card 40 features Nick Cravat in the series according to its reverse, though the image on the card is in actuality George Dolenz as the Count and Max Brimmell who appeared in several episodes.

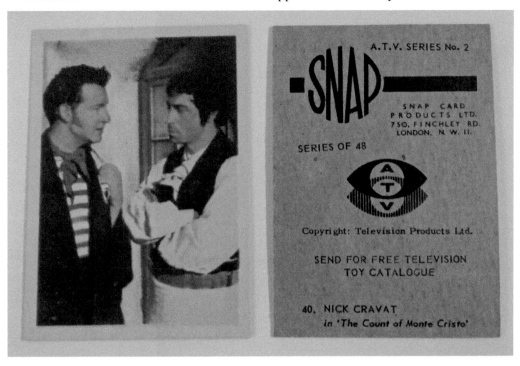

ATV Stars card 40 showing George Dolenz, not Nick Cravat as stated on card.

Sir Francis Drake

This was the last swashbuckling show produced for ITC. Debuting in 1961, the series starred Terence Morgan as Sir Francis Drake, the sixteenth-century maritime adventurer, with Jean Kent as Elizabeth I. Another regular in the series is John Drake, his nephew and cabin boy, played by Michael Crawford.

Much filming took place around Brixham in Devon, where a full-size replica of Drake's ship the *Golden Hind* was built upon a former motor fishing vessel. This reconstruction, designed by Hugh Paget, was based on an illustration of the *Golden Hind* featured on the old halfpenny coin. This ship remained moored in Brixham long after the show had finished, becoming home to a museum about Drake. Sadly while on the way to Southampton for a refit in the mid-eighties this original replica sank in bad weather. A replacement was constructed and is now moored in its place.

Taking orders directly from Queen Elizabeth, Drake was a lone wolf and expert swordsman, who loyally defended queen and country from foreign invaders throughout the twenty-six half-hour episodes. Several of these adventures involved thwarting the plots of the Spanish ambassador, Mendoza, played by future *Doctor Who* star Roger Delgardo, while still maintaining diplomatic relations and avoiding war with Spain.

Books

The annual *ATV Television Show Book 1961* had a small feature on *Sir Francis Drake*; a near full page photograph of Terence Morgan and Jean Kent, with a small passage of text beneath. The series fared better in *Girl Television and Film Annual 1963* from Hulton Press, with a three-page feature with photographs entitled 'The "Halfpenny" ship – and the people who sail in her'. As with other series featured in this book, a painting book was produced and published by GFS (Black & Stratton). While the *London Illustrated News* published a one-page photographic feature in its 23 September 1961 issue.

Sir Francis Drake feature from the *ATV Television Show Book 1961.*

Painting book. (Steven Taylor)

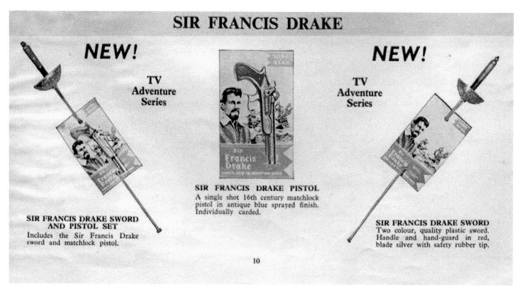

SIR FRANCIS DRAKE

NEW!

TV
Adventure
Series

NEW!

TV
Adventure
Series

SIR FRANCIS DRAKE PISTOL
A single shot 16th century matchlock pistol in antique blue sprayed finish. Individually carded.

SIR FRANCIS DRAKE SWORD
AND PISTOL SET
Includes the Sir Francis Drake sword and matchlock pistol.

SIR FRANCIS DRAKE SWORD
Two colour, quality plastic sword. Handle and hand-guard in red, blade silver with safety rubber tip.

10

Sir Francis Drake range in 1962 Lone Star catalogue.

Toys

The UK toy company Lone Star introduced three products for *Sir Francis Drake* into its range in 1962. There was a toy sword described in the catalogue as 'Two colour, quality sword in strong pliable plastic. Handle and hand guard in red, blade silver with safety rubber tip'. This remained in their range until 1966. The second was an 'antique blue sprayed finished' toy pistol based on a sixteenth-century matchlock. Both of these items came individually carded, but were also packaged as a pair to become the third product for the show. The backing cards for all three products appear to have the same design – an illustration of Drake to the left with sailing ships in the distance behind and to the right. Both the pistol and duel set disappeared from the range in 1964.

Tower Press produced a jigsaw based on the series entitled 'Fight for the Treasure' in its second series of TV jigsaws in 1961. Other jigsaws in this series were for shows like *Sea Hunt* and *Overland Trail.*

Trading Cards

In 1961 in the UK A&BC Gum issued a set of twenty-five large colour photographs from the series with bubble gum. In 1962 Terence Morgan featured on cards 9 and 25 in the Mister Softee *TV Personalities* set.

Right: A&BC
card set.

Below: Mister
Softee cards 25
and 9.

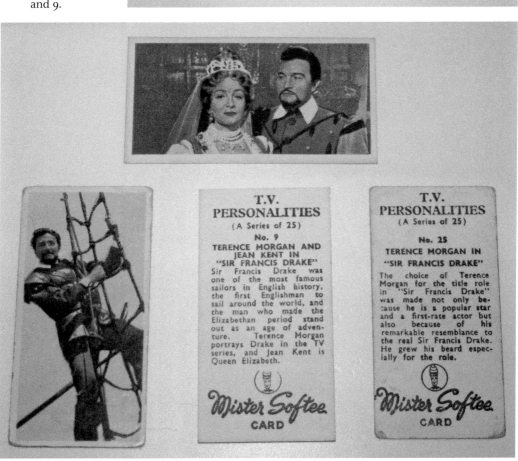

Records

Two versions of the *Sir Frances Drake* theme were released as singles in 1961. The first was by Ivor Slaney and his Orchestra on HMV (45-POP 943). The second was by the Piccadilly Strings on the Piccadilly label (7N.35013).

The Ivor Slaney recording appears on Brazilian EP *Melodias da Televisao* (Odeon 7ID – 4073) around 1962, which also included the themes from *Danger Man*, *Dr Kildare* and *Highway Patrol*.

HMV released *Your Favourite TV and Radio Themes* (HMV CLP1565) in 1962, which also contains the Ivor Slaney recording.

HMV theme single.

HMV theme
single
demo disc.

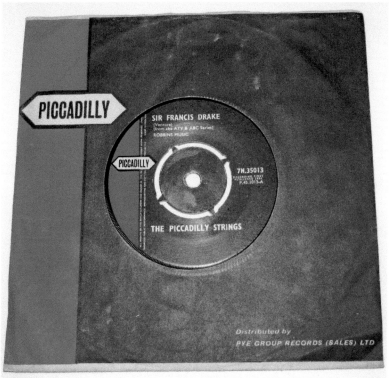

Theme single,
Piccadilly.

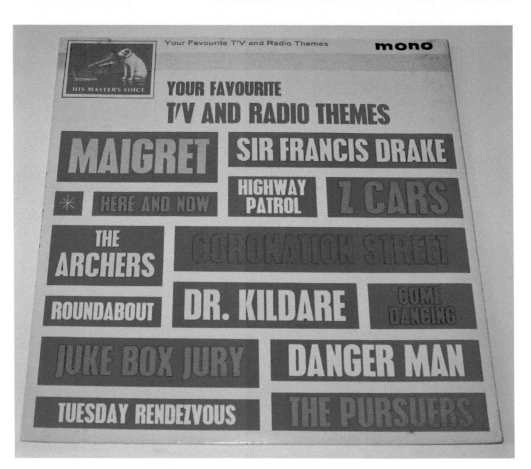

Your Favourite TV and Radio Themes LP.

Sword of Freedom

Produced by Sapphire Films for ITC, and running for thirty-nine episodes, the series follows the adventures of Marco Del Monte (Edmund Purdom) a freedom-loving painter and skilled swordsman who would defend the people of fifteenth-century Florence against the tyrannical Medicis. Series regulars included the delightful Adrienne Corri as Angelica the reformed pickpocket, now Del Monte's model, Rowland Bartrop as Sandro, and Martin Benson as a suitably devious Duke de Medici, while Kenneth Hyde portrayed the duplicitous Machiavelli.

Books
In the 1958 *Girl Film and Television Annual Number 2*, publishers Hulton Press included a photographic feature written by Adrienne Corri about Edmund Purdom and working on the series.

Trading Cards
While it did not get its own set of trading cards, six cards appear in other sets that are of interest. These come from four different larger sets featuring images from several television series. In *ATV Stars series 1*, by Snap Card Products, card 36 of fifty features Adrienne Corri and Edmund Purdom.

 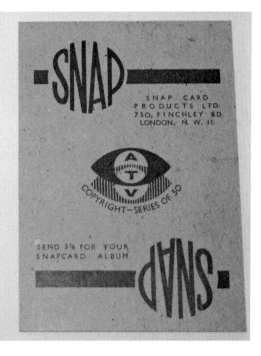

Snap card 36, featuring *Sword of Freedom*.

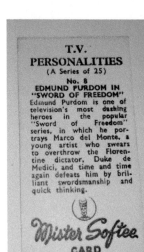

Left: Mister Softee card 8.

Below: *Who-z-at Star* cards 12 and 51.

Who-z-at Star card 21.

Cards of interest in the *Who-z-at Star* set published by A&BC Gum are card 12 featuring Edmond Purdom on the front, card 51 featuring Martin Benson on its front with reference to Edmund Purdom on the back, and also card 21 featuring the Peters' sisters with Martin Benson referenced on the rear. Card 8 in the Mister Softee *TV Personalities* set features Edmund Purdom. Also the unnumbered 1961 A&BC Gum *Fotostars* set features Edmond Purdom as Marco on one card.

Magazines/Comics

The only products directly related to the series would appear to be four small comic books from the publishers Pearson's *TV Picture Stories* series. The first of these, *Vendetta*, appeared in February of 1959. March 1959 saw the next two, *Adriana* and *Violetta*. The final title released was *The Assassin*, appearing in June 1959. All four are based on episodes of the TV series.

The Midlands region *TV Times* featured *Sword of Freedom* on the cover of the issue dated 4 July 1958, showing Edmund Purdom and Adrienne Corri in Marco's studio.

Sword of Freedom: Vendetta comic.

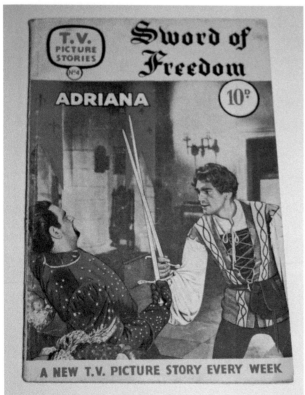

Sword of Freedom: Adriana comic.

Sword of Freedom: Violetta comic.

Sword of Freedom: The Assassin comic.
(Steven Taylor)

TV Times cover.

William Tell

Fourteenth-century Switzerland. The country is under Austrian rule, and one man dares to stand against the tyrannical regime. Conrad Phillips plays the legendary Swiss bowman in this 1950s adaptation of the legend. It's really little more than a Swiss version of Robin Hood, with Willoughby Goddard's character of Gressler (the Austrian governor) representing the Sheriff of Nottingham. Thirty-nine episodes were produced in the popular half-hour format used by ITC.

Books

In 1959 Adprint produced a William Tell annual containing mostly text stories, adapted by Terence Walker from the TV series. The annual cost 7/6d and was illustrated by G.A. Embleton.

Adprint produced a similar book in 1960. This was simply *William Tell Adventure Stories*. While G.A. Embleton once again produced the artwork, writing duties fell to David Leader.

William Tell also featured in Adprint's 1958 *ATV Show Book*, in an article entitled 'Film Series' and again with a feature in their 1959 *ATV Television Show Book*.

Purnell's 1959 *ATV Television Star Book* includes a feature on William Tell, as does their 1960 *ATV Television Show Book*.

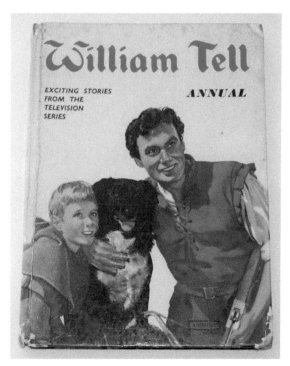

William Tell annual.

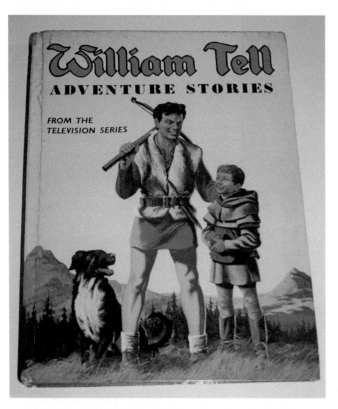

William Tell Adventure Stories.

Painting book.

A William Tell painting book was published by Black & Stratton Ltd. This cheaply produced book contains illustrations by John Martin, while the *No. 1 Dotto Book* contains puzzles based on the show.

Toys/Games

Bell Toys produced a William Tell jigsaw puzzle in 1960. This was entitled 'Suspense'. The scene showed William and Hedda hiding in the bushes from Landburgeher Gessler and his soldiers. Sized approximately 17 x 11 inches, this was originally sold in a two-piece box with a lift-off lid, but was later reissued, design unchanged, in an end-opening thinner single-piece box. At this time a second William Tell jigsaw puzzle was produced. This much scarcer item depicts the famous scene of William Tell shooting the apple from his son's head.

Jigsaw two-piece style box.

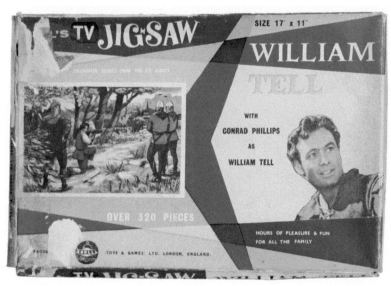

Second issue jigsaw. (Ralph Cooper)

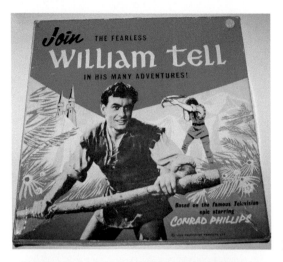

Bell Toys board game.

Playing board for board game.

Original artboard for DiBro Crossbow
box lid.

A board game was also produced for the series by Bell Toys in 1959. It is a fairly simple game involving a chase across the Swiss Alps, with the winner being the first player to get three men into Landburgeher's castle. Its colourful board features a central revolving piece representing secret ways through the forest, randomly turned according to dice throws.

DiBro Ltd produced a William Tell crossbow shooting range, which consisted of a small plastic crossbow, with four suction-tipped bolts, along with colourful targets showing Gessler and his men.

Trading Cards

In 1960 the British company A&BC Gum produced a set of thirty-six cards, the *Exploits of William Tell*. These cards have colour photographs from the series. While the set is declared as thirty-six cards, there is a card 37. This card is just a repeat of card 7; same image, same text – just numbered 37.

Buster comic gave away with issues a set of twelve cards entitled *Men of Danger*. Card 9 was a photograph of Conrad Phillips as William Tell.

The *Who-z-at Star* set of cards from A&BC Gum has five cards of interest. Card number 36 features Conrad Phillips in the role. He is also referenced on the back of card 52, which featured Willoughby Goddard as Landburgher Gessler, who is also referenced on the back of card 20, Lena Horne. Card 5 features Jennifer Jayne as Hedda Tell, also referenced on the back of card 48, Peggy Mount.

The two parallel Dotto card sets by Snap Card Products featured both Conrad Phillips on cards 16, and Willoughby Goddard on cards 12 of the sets. Again from Snap Card Products, card 7 in *ATV Stars series 1* featured both Conrad Phillips and Willoughby Goddard.

ABC cinemas gave members of the ABC minors club a large full colour postcard of the series in 1958.

A&BC Gum set.

Above left: A&BC Gum variant card, reverse.

Above right: Card from *Buster* comic.

Above left: *Who-z-at Star* cards 36 and 5.

Above right: *Who-z-at Star* card 52.

Above left: Who-z-at Star cards 20 and 48.

Above right: Dotto cards.

Above left: ATV stars card 7.

Above right: ABC Minors large-sized postcard.

Comics

Pearson produced a series of digest-sized comics under the title *TV Picture Stories* and several featured William Tell. *The Assassins* appeared in February 1959. His next appearances were in March with *The Bear* and *The Prisoner*.

Pearson produced two other William Tell comics in 1960. These were in the larger American comic book size, in its short-lived *TV Photo Stories* comic. The stories featured were *The Killer* and *The Young Widow*. Unlike the *TV Picture Stories* that featured traditional drawn illustrations, these *TV Photo Stories* comics are compiled of photographs from the series. All comics appear to be based upon television series episodes of the same name. One issue of *Guillermo Tell* appeared in Spain – possibly a reprint of a Pearson comic.

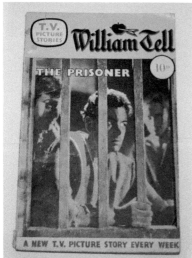

Above: William Tell: The Assassins comic and *William Tell: The Bear* comic.

Left: William Tell: The Prisoner comic.

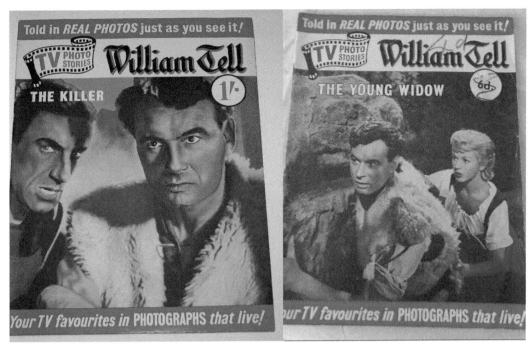

William Tell TV Photo Library *The Killer* and *The Young Widow*. (Ralph Cooper)

William Tell: The Killer comic, inside pages.

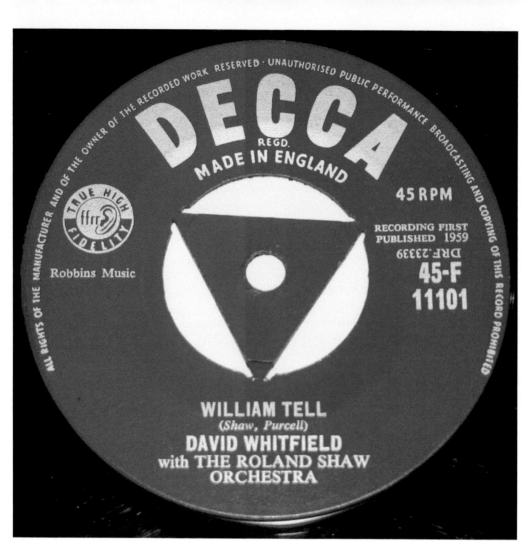

Theme single.

Records

The series theme song, based upon the 'William Tell Overture' by Gioachino Rossini, was released as a single by David Whitfield with the Roland Shaw Orchestra, in 1959 on the Decca label. (45-F 11101)

Miscellaneous

Huntley & Palmers produced a round biscuit tin with a photograph on its lid for William Tell in 1958.

Postcards appeared in France, where the series was known as *Guillaume Tell*, as part of a series of postcards titled *Heros de la Television*.

Two 35 mm Film Stips sets were issued featuring photographic images from the series entitled *William Tell and the Apple* and *William Tell and the Raid*.

Biscuit tin.

French postcard.

William Tell and the Apple film strip. (Ralph Cooper)

Postscript

Being over sixty years since any of the series in this book were produced, many items featured are incredibly rare, and it is highly probable that many directly related to these series have indeed been omitted due to not being discovered or known about during the research and writing of this book. In fact, several items did come to light too late to be included, such as a plaster moulding set for Robin Hood and William Tell peanut butter glasses. If you do know of any omissions, the author can be contacted via the Little Storping Museum website: www.murdersville.co.uk/museum.

Acknowledgements
I would like to thank the following for their assistance in the preparation of this book: Steven Taylor, Bruce Button, Louise Harker at Vectis Toy Auctions, Remco Admiraal, Robert Girling, Ralph Cooper, and Stephen Brown. In addition, the Little Storping Museum. Finally, thanks to William Woodward for his help and proofreading skills.